e-Business
Essentials

Time-saving books that teach specific skills to busy people, focusing on what really matters; the things that make a difference – the *essentials*.

Other books in the series include:

Writing Business E-mails

Create Great Spreadsheets

Getting Started on the Internet

Job Hunt on the Net

Business Communication

Solving Problems

Delegating

Writing Great Copy

Other How To Books by Bruce Durie

Creating a Web Site

1000 Best Web Sites

Quick Fix Your Web Life

Quick Fix Your Mobile Phone

For full details please send for a free copy of the latest catalogue. See back cover for address.

e-Business
Essentials

Bruce Durie

ESSENTIALS

Published in 2001 by
How To Books Ltd, 3 Newtec Place,
Magdalen Road, Oxford OX4 1RE, United Kingdom
Tel: (01865) 793806   Fax: (01865) 248780
e-mail: info@howtobooks.co.uk
www.howtobooks.co.uk

British Library Cataloguing in Publication Data.
A catalogue record for this book is available from
the British Library.

Edited by Diana Brueton
Cover design by Shireen Nathoo Design
Produced for How To Books by Deer Park Productions
Typeset by PDQ Typesetting, Newcastle-under-Lyme, Staffordshire
Printed and bound in Great Britain by Bell & Bain Ltd, Glasgow

NOTE: The material contained in this book is set out in good faith for
general guidance and no liability can be accepted for loss or expense
incurred as a result of relying in particular circumstances on
statements made in the book. Laws and regulations are complex
and liable to change, and readers should check the current position
with the relevant authorities before making personal arrangements.

ESSENTIALS *is an imprint of*
How To Books

Contents

Essential information

Glossary

see *http:www.e-business.essentials.com/*
essentials/glossary.htm

Note: all URLs and e-mail addresses are correct at the time of writing, but may change. Consult http://www.e-business-essentials.com for changes.

Introduction: What is e-Business?

Is this you?

• You want to be able to sell products or services on the Internet. • You want better electronic business-to-business communication. • If you don't do it, your competitors will. • You know that there is a great deal of help, advice, guidance, free or subsidised consultancy and many local events. • You feel a lot of this is partial, useless or wrong. • It is still very hard to know where to start. • You are bewildered by it all.

You could:

~ Hire an expensive consultant on a daily basis.

~ Buy a complete solution (software and hardware) from someone.

~ Try to assemble the software, hardware, knowledge and expertise yourself.

Whichever of these options you choose, this book is intended to help by giving you enough information to make an informed

choice. And don't forget to visit
http://www.e-business-essentials.com/

e-Business is not just e-commerce

'e-commerce' means any electronic way of processing financial transactions, either between businesses and the public (customers) or business to business. For instance:

~ Electronic share transactions.

~ Electronic Data Interchange (EDI) such as barcode readers in shops.

~ Automated Teller Machines (ATM) cash dispensers.

~ On-line banking – control bank accounts from your computer.

~ Taking (or giving) credit card information via the Internet or Web for B2C (business to consumer) translations.

~ Electronic procurement, invoicing and payment for B2B (business to business) transactions.

But e-Business is more than that –
e-commerce is a vital part of e-Business, but
not the only part. As well as some of the
e-commerce elements above, the other crucial
components of e-Business are:

~ Organising your general business processes
using computers and other electronic or
telecommunications devices.

~ Managing your supplier chain.

~ Managing your customer relationships
(including marketing).

~ Managing your stock, production,
procurement, workflow and shipping
electronically.

The Internet and the Web

The world wide Web ('the Web') is only a part
of the Internet.

The Internet is a network of computers
which uses phone lines, cables and exchanges
to share information. It includes:

~ e-mail or electronic mail for transfer of text
messages.

~ Newsgroups and bulletin boards which allow sharing of information via a network of newsgroups called the Usenet.

~ Internet Relay Chat (IRC) for synchronous communication between users, by keyboard or voice.

~ File Transfer Protocol (FTP) and other ways of uploading (sending to a server) or downloading (getting from a server) files, documents, programs and other resources.

The Web is a graphical enhancement of text-only Internet, allowing:

~ hypertext markup language (HTML) for control of fonts, colours etc

~ hyperlinks (click on a word or image and load another page)

~ inclusion of dynamic text, video, audio, graphics etc

~ integration of e-mail, newsgroups, IRC, FTP and other Internet components into Web pages.

The Internet means that any business can become an e-Business.

Properly implemented, e-Business can use all these Internet components for better business*

All of this has become possible because of the wide availability of:

~ Web browser programs (such as Netscape and Internet Explorer)

~ easy-to-use e-mail clients (Eudora, Pegasus, Outlook Express etc)

~ cheap computer hardware

~ changes to the telephone system allowing faster data transmission (ISDN, ADSL etc)

~ a vast range of free, or cheap and easy to use software allowing most people to do almost anything they want.

1 What e-Business Means for You

e-Business means the combination of three sets of activities.

1   **Internal business processes** – your business could be handled better, faster or cheaper with the right technology. For instance:
    ~ Do all your co-workers use the same contact databases?
    ~ Do they *have* contact databases, or is everything on bits of paper?
    ~ Are your accounts on your computer?
    ~ If so, do they link to any spreadsheets or databases you use for business planning and monitoring?
    ~ Do you *do* any business planning or monitoring?
    ~ Is there any connection at all between you and others by voice, memos, hand-written notes and meetings at the coffee machine?

2   **Customer and supplier relationships** – advertising, marketing, customer support, customer contact, order processing and

delivery scheduling can be managed with the right software, hardware and organisation.*

3 **e-commerce** – ordering, managing and paying for items, selling products and services over the Internet and receiving payment.

The advantages of e-Business

The widespread adoption of the Internet and the Web means that all businesses can now:

~ **Operate globally** – you are not restricted to customers who walk past your shop window, see your listing in directories or the local paper or get your leaflet by mail.

~ **Expand the customer base** – any other business or private individual with access to the Internet is a potential customer.

~ **Compete effectively** – your existing competitors and even more new ones you never knew you had are taking this very seriously.

~ **Process orders, payments and deliveries**

* *This book concentrates on the use of the Internet for these business processes, but they must integrate with other activities you undertake.*

automatically – all the normal business processes can be streamlined.

~ **Advertise widely** – global brand development is now possible.

~ **Focus the marketing effort** – building up profiles of your current and potential customers for more targeted approaches.

~ **Cut costs** – streamline your processes and save money.

~ **Integrate your business activities** – pull together all the things you do using computers and telecommunications.

You're already doing e-Business

You are probably using a number of e-Business tools. For example you:

~ confirm an order by phone or fax

~ send a customer or a supplier an e-mail

~ keep your accounts, customer details, supplier database and stock records on a computer

~ have a Web site

~ regularly check your competition's Web sites

~ use the Web to research markets and products.

Now ask yourself:

~ How many of these do you do?
~ How well do you do them?
~ How integrated are they?
~ What else could you do, or do better?

2 Essential Resources – Motivation and Time

e-Business is a threat to some

It takes resources and courage to challenge existing business. On the Internet a lot of the barriers have gone. Who is threatened?

~ Car dealerships – get a car direct from the manufacturer, or find one in Europe and ship it home with the paperwork.

~ Travel agents – choose a holiday, get flights, hotel, car hire, tickets to attractions and insurance on your PC at 3 am.

~ Computer stores – buy on-line and have it delivered.

~ Banks – organise your finances from home.

~ Music and video shops – download an audio or video clip, download the entire MP3 file or order the CD or DVD.

~ Book shops – you can get most books faster, cheaper and with greater choice.

~ Education – learn a language, improve your computer skills, take a diploma, using on-line and distance learning.

~ Design and print houses – forget expensive, glossy brochures.

e-Business is no threat to you

On the Internet no one knows how big or small you are. Global sales opportunities are as far away as your keyboard. One or a few people can start, manage and grow a successful operation.*

Have you thought through the alternatives to *not* doing e-Business and the pitfalls?

Reasons to do e-Business

A business can become regional, national or global more easily, cheaper and faster by doing e-Business. At present, how do you:

~ Update your catalogue, price list, contact details and brochures?

~ Collect payments?

* *The Web can turn us all into "netrepreneurs".*

~ Keep track of paper every day, week, month, year?

~ Make it easy for customers to deal with you?

~ Spend less time talking to people who never become customers?

~ Collect information on customers?

~ Contact your entire customer base?

~ Do business with companies doing e-Business?

~ Integrate your sales information with your customer database?

~ Aim to provide additional services?

Reasons *not* to do e-Business

If any of these worry you, address them before you start your e-Business, or at least think about the implications.

~ Can you keep your promises? If you sell something to Australia can you get it there, on schedule and in one piece?

~ Can you trade in different countries and currencies?

~ Is what you sell, advertise or provide legal

in every country?

~ Does e-Business fit with your existing business model or should you develop a new one?

~ Are all your customers or suppliers on-line?

~ If not, do you want them as customers or suppliers?

~ Can you trade in foreign languages?

~ How will your e-Business stand out against the millions of business Web sites, on-line stores and Internet adverts out there already?

~ Are you organised to take advantage of Internet opportunities?

What's to gain?

~ You can make and receive payments electronically.

~ You can expand into new markets.

~ You don't need a huge advertising and promotions budget.

~ Your 'static' Web site can do most of your

work if upgraded.

~ You can spend more time on your business and less time on trivia.

The best e-Businesses

Some business models adapt to e-Business more easily than others, chiefly those which:

~ sell easily-shipped produce
~ have a simple catalogue or product list
~ sell information
~ offer customer support by telephone.*

How much time will it take?

Your e-Business can be largely created in spare time. Most of the hard work is thinking and planning.

Your first step is to write a business plan. If you have never done this before, there are many business aids free on-line which can help you. Brunel University has links to business startup resources (*http://sol.brunel.ac. uk/~jarvis/bola.businesses/busplan/*) as does the American Small Business Administration

* Almost any business can adopt e-Business practices and gain from them.

(*http://www.sba.gov/*) but there are many others.*

If you were presenting your idea to a bank manager:

~ How would you explain it in a few sentences?

~ How would you promote it?

~ What are the opportunities and can you quantify them?

~ What is it going to cost?

~ What is the competition?

~ What questions would you be asked?

~ What will the revenue be?

You may have existing business tools which you would like to build into your e-Business such as:

~ customer support
~ discussion forum
~ e-mail
~ fax
~ mail-order
~ catalogue

~ data sheets
~ drawings and diagrams
~ existing web site
~ information packs
~ news releases

* *Search for "Business Plan Software" in any search engine.*

~   newsletters   ~   product brochures.

If you don't have e-mail, see page 37. If you don't have a Web site, see page 61.

3 Essential Resources – Your Computer

To do e-Business you will need the following equipment and software:

~ Hardware – a computer, capable of connecting to the Internet and powerful enough to run the programs you will need. By preference it should be a PC running Windows 95, 98, ME or 2000.
~ Dial-up software.
~ An e-mail program.
~ A Web browser.
~ A news reader program.
~ An FTP client.
~ A connection to the Internet.
~ An account with an Internet Service Provider (ISP).

Choosing your hardware

Your computer should ideally be at least the following specification

~ Pentium II or III (or equivalent) PC
~ 200MB hard disc

~ CD-ROM

~ decent graphics card

~ colour monitor 17-inch or larger

~ at least 250MHz CPU (500 is better)

~ 64K of RAM

~ modem (see below)

~ full duplex sound card

~ keyboard and mouse.

The type of PC sold in high street or mail
order outlets for under £1,000 should suffice.
Make sure it has (or upgrade to) Windows 98
or 2000 as your operating system otherwise
your options will be limited. Most modern
Internet and Web software is designed to run
under Windows 95 and/or 98. Not all are Win
2000 compatible.

Modem

Your modem should be 56K flex fax/voice/
data so that you can send faxes as well as
Internet data. If you have to buy one, get an
external modem. This will make it easier to
change if you decide to install ISDN (see
below).*

* See Modem tips
  (p 35).

~ **ISDN** – this uses the same phone lines but
is about twice as fast. Usually two digital

lines are available, so it can be four times as fast if you use both, but you pay for two phone calls.*

~ **ADSL or Cable Modem** – these options are faster than ISDN and may come bundled with your telephone or television service.

~ **Leased lines** – an established business may choose to install a leased line. This is no faster than ISDN but is 'open' all the time and has no call charges. It will cost several thousand pounds per year and also needs specialised router equipment. This is an option if you plan to operate your own server and need a permanent connection, or if there is to be a lot of large data transfer – an architectural or design practice, or a software-selling business, for instance.

Which? All in all, 56K is fine for those starting out, with ISDN as an option (especially for established businesses) and ADSL will suit most people. Cable modem is fast and reliable, and becoming cheaper.

* *See ISDN Tips (p 35).*

Choosing your software

Dial-up software

If you have Windows 95 or 98, you will already have TCP/IP. You will also need Dial-Up networking (in your **My Computer** desktop icon). When you choose an ISP the configuring software may do the hard work for you. Alternatively, there is an Internet Connection Wizard at **Start, Programs, Accessories, Communications**.

An e-mail program

Microsoft Internet Explorer 4 or 5 comes with an e-mail client called Outlook Express. Netscape Communicator has Netscape Mail. These are fine for most business purposes. Other popular e-mail clients such as Pegasus or Eudora operate much the same way.

There are two common mail protocols:

~ SMTP (Simple Mail Transfer Protocol) is for receiving
~ POP3 (Post Office Protocol 3) for sending.*

Usually your ISP's mail server will be called something like *mail.isp.co.uk* but do check.

* See page 41 for more detail.

A Web browser

Microsoft Internet Explorer (latest version IE5) and Netscape Communicator (latest version 4.7 or 6.0) are the commonest. Have both installed so you can test your Web site for compatibility with each.

If you sign up with an ISP, you may be offered IE5 (and Outlook Express) or Netscape on the CD or as part of the download. If not, they are widely available free on the front of PC magazines or by downloading from Microsoft and Netscape respectively.

There is no harm in overwriting your existing installations with these as you can change the **Options** (and remove the irritating logos) later.

A news reader program

There are over 40,000 newsgroups, some of which will be a useful source of information for your business and a valuable advertising mechanism. News Readers are included with IE4 or IE5 (as part of Outlook Express) but Internet News is also available free and is built into Netscape Communicator. Your ISP will have a news server called *news.isp.co.uk* or similar – check for the correct name.

An FTP client

File Transfer Protocol (FTP) is the commonest
way to download and upload files. Both IE5
and Netscape come with a Publisher (a
dedicated FTP client) and FrontPage (page
94) has its own Publisher. But you may wish
to get a more flexible program – FTP
Voyager, WS-FTP or CuteFTP. Often a Web site
– especially one which features downloads –
will have a dedicated FTP server, usually
called something like *ftp.isp.co.uk* as distinct
from *www.isp.co.uk*, the main Web site.

Choosing your ISP

An ISP (Internet Service Provider) is a gateway
to the Internet. At the very least they provide
a dial-up number. Many also offer software
set-up programs (CD or download) and e-mail
access. Some provide free or cheap Web
space. Your Web domain and your e-mail will
be a variant of theirs (*mydomain.thisisp.co.uk*)
and *j.smith@mydomain.thisip.co.uk*).

   Free ISPs usually require that you install a

customised browser with their logo, enter via a home page loaded with adverts, have cookies enabled (so they can get information about you) and have Caller Line ID forwarding so they know who you are. In many cases these are companies which previously were not in the Internet business, such as Tesco, Virgin, Boots, WH Smith etc – in other words, *they have become e-Businesses*. And if they can do it, why shouldn't you?*

Choose

A business should have an account with a full-service ISP, after establishing its own domain name. If e-mail is not provided, ask about e-mail forwarding. They may also have useful on-line databases – company searches, shares information and business newsgroups. There is no harm in having free or cheap dial-up and e-mail from a free ISP as well. Sign up with Freeserve, TescoNet or another free service to get started.

A new e-Business is going to need:

~ A 'real' domain name (not *jim.somefreebie. co.uk*)

~ 'Real' e-mail (not *jim@jim.somefreebie.co.uk*)

* *There are also full-service ISPs whose business is providing commercial Web space, e-mail and other services for real Web sites.*

~ 'Real' Web space (where e-commerce can be run).

This is all available free or very cheaply.

Subvert your free ISP

Your free Internet CD is installed, your e-mail address is *marymack@freethingy.com* and you have 10MB of Web space waiting at *www.marymack.freethingy.com*.

1   Remove the 'Supplied by FreeThingy' banner and logo on the Internet Explorer. Go to Program Files/Internet Explorer and delete a sub-folder called SIGNUP or rename it (eg $IGNUP).

2   Instead of the Freethingy home page, open your browser, find one you prefer – AltaVista (*http://www.altavista.co.uk/*) for instance – then:
    ~ Netscape 4: Click **Edit, Preferences, Navigator, Navigator starts with Home Page, Use current page**.
    ~ IE4: Click **View, Internet Options, General, Home Page, Use Current**.
    ~ IE5: Click **Tools, Internet Options, General, Home Page, Use Current**.

You can still use their free dial-up number.

3   Once you have established your own domain and Web space elsewhere, have one page on the FreeThingy site with nothing but a link saying 'Site moved to *http://www.marymack.co.uk*' and a clickable link or a redirection.

4   Have all other e-mail you set up later (*mary@marymack.co.uk*) forwarded to the Freethingy one by your other ISP.

Free dial-up, domains, Web space, e-mail etc

One good option is to sign up with ConnectFree. Either:

1   Go to *http://www.connectfree.co.uk* and click on Free Internet. This can provide you with a dial-up number (including ISDN), a domain of the form *http://www. mydomain.connectfree.co.uk*, Web space and e-mail like *helen@mydomain. connectfree.co.uk*. This may be a useful 'first' account, for home and personal use, say. Follow the procedures and print out

all pages with information on host names, passwords etc.

2   Alternatively, go to *http://www.connectfree.co.uk/* and click on Free Domains. This can only register domains with .co.uk or .org suffixes (not .com). Check whether your chosen domain name is available at *http://www.nominet.net/whois.html* (Fig. 2, p 76). Print out any useful information pages. FreeDomNames requires a two-to-three minute phone call to set up the domain at £1.50 per minute, and a £5 per two years ongoing registration fee. It takes one to two working days for registration. Then set up your Web space at *http://signup.freedomnames.co.uk/updates/*. This service also supports FrontPage 2000 (for more adventurous Web page designers), e-commerce and ADSL.

Free phone calls

Phone and cable companies offer free calls or a very cheap rate:*

~ BT's SurfTime – a monthly charge of about £20 ($30).

* *There may be even better, cheaper or free deals available.*

~ Telewest's Surf Unlimited – £10 per month ($15) plus an agreement to spend at least £10 a month on your other line. You may get these combined with your telephone or TV service.

Essential modem tips

Modems use the standard telephone line to communicate. The '56K' refers to the maximum speed (57,600 bits per second) your modem can transfer data. In practice speeds are slower so a 1MB file will take about four to ten minutes to download.

To minimise cost and time spent waiting, do your downloads and uploads when no one else is. Calls are cheaper after 6pm or 8pm and at weekends. America wakes up in the early afternoon UK time so the Internet is slow until at least 10pm.*

Essential ISDN Tips

ISDN is a time-saver and a potential money-saver if you plan to do large uploads and downloads, but it is expensive. This will

* *Other bottlenecks occur at 7-8 am and 6-8 pm.*

change with the increased popularity of cable modems – available from your phone and/or TV cable company.

If you do decide to use ISDN, make sure your ISP supports it, or change to one which can. There are also deals for people who change to or from cable providers or BT. There are also loyalty deals for *not* changing.

ADSL may be even cheaper than ISDN, but it may not yet be available in your area.

4 Essential e-Mail

Advantages of e-mail

E-mail is your greatest business resource.

1   E-mail is almost free – all it costs is your time and a phone call.
2   Since you can send one e-mail to many recipients, this is an incredibly cost-effective business tool.
3   There is practically no delay in sending and receiving e-mails.
4   A properly worded e-mail can't be misunderstood the way a non-recorded phone call can.
5   You have a record of what you sent, to whom and when.
6   It takes the fax a logical step further – no paper.
7   The message can be amended and edited.
8   E-mail-to-fax programs allow you to reach fax machines.
9   Pictures can be sent by e-mail at their existing resolutions as can audio, video and practically any other form of digitised

information.

10 You can set up your e-mail client to filter or exclude 'spam'.

11 E-mail can be automated – you can forward e-mails to another location when you are elsewhere, set up an automatic response to say you are on holiday, notify you of e-mails received, log in from other places to receive your messages and so on.

Disadvantages of e-mail

Treat e-mail as a welcome extension to business communications and a time-saver, not as a welcome extension to social life and a time-waster. Make these rules for your staff (and yourself!).

1 All meetings and company memos will be notified by e-mail *only*.

2 Everyone should check their e-mails three times a day.

3 When a message is received check who it's from, what it's about and deal with it when appropriate, just as with a paper message.

4 Scrutinise all e-mail logs weekly to stop gossiping.
5 E-mail is a business tool and the contents are property of the employer, just like business letters or the company's telephone.*

Your e-mail address

There are three main ways to get an e-mail address.

1 Your ISP will provide you with one. For instance, a Compuserve user will have an address like *anderson@compuserve.com*
2 Free Web-based e-mail is available from many Internet companies such as Yahoo, Netscape or Microsoft. The address is like *billy@yahoo.com*. It can be accessed from any computer through a browser – all you need is your log-in name (username) and password. This is handy for people on the move. You have to be on-line to compose and reply to e-mails.
3 If you have your own domain name you can get an e-mail address with the domain. This may be a true POP3 e-mail

* *The occasional personal call or e-mail is a privilege, not a right.*

address or an 'alias' for e-mail forwarding. For instance, ConnectFree will provide you with up to five real, separate e-mail addresses of the type *yourname@yourbit.connectfree.co.uk*. A full-service ISP may give you one e-mail address with your domain but any mail to the domain –

> *info@yourdomain.co.uk*,
> *sales@yourdomain.co.uk*
> *jim.jones@yourdomain.co.uk*

all come to one mailbox. It looks like your business has staff and departments.

Filtering messages

You can use the name before the @ sign in e-mail addresses to tell you what the source was and filter messages into different mailboxes.

Three examples of how this can be useful:

1   You buy something on-line and they send you sales e-mails for evermore dressed up as Marketing Tips or offers. Give your e-mail address as *rubbish@yourdomain.co.uk*, and set your e-mail program to block any mail to that address.

2   When setting up a Web site for a client
    (say, Chester Chocs) include an e-mail link
    to *chchocs@yourdomain.co.uk* so users
    can notify you, as Webmaster, of any
    problems with the site. You know from
    the incoming address to look at it and fix
    if necessary.

3   Small companies can use the 'five free
    e-mail addresses' offer of free ISPs to
    good effect. If you really have five
    employees, each can have an e-mail
    address. If it's just you, set up addresses
    like

    sales@myplace.freeisp.co.uk
    info@myplace.freeisp.co.uk
    feedback@myplace.freeisp.co.uk

    and others to make you look larger than
    you are. If you have only one 'real' e-mail
    address use e-mail forwarding so that
    addresses like *sales@...*, *accounts@...* will
    all be forwarded to your single 'real'
    address.

Using POP3 and SMTP

Most modern e-mail programs and ISPs use

POP3 for incoming mail (receiving) and SMTP for outgoing mail (sending). POP3 accesses mail on a post office or mail server, and SMTP is used to communicate between a computer and a 'post office' server. Using SMTP to receive mail, the system thinks it is communicating with another post office, not an individual computer, and *all* mail for a certain domain will come to that computer – so *john@ourplace.com* and *janet@ourplace.com* will be identical to the system and anyone will get everyone's mail.*

With POP3 for receiving, each e-mail address requires a separate log-in. John and Janet will get their own mail, not each other's.

If you have set up addresses like *sales@ourplace.com*, *infor@ourplace.com* etc and they're really all just you, or you want to see them all, have all of them in your e-mail program's Accounts and your e-mail client POP3 will sweep each one in turn when you log on.

Many ISPs use both, so your chosen e-mail client should be able to handle both. Some ISPs (Demon is an example) use only SMTP,

* *Remember that the first person who downloads an e-mail message effectively prevents anyone else from getting it.*

so you will need an e-mail program capable of supporting SMTP for both receive and send.

This can complicate life for multiple-user domains but simplify it for a single user with multiple addresses.

Intranets and networks

If you want to give everyone on your organisation's network the ability to use e-mail over the Internet, you will need a multi-user account from your ISP. You may in future, so check it is an option.

If your office network has a mail system installed for internal communication – eg Microsoft Mail (comes with networked Windows) – this can also be used for Internet e-mail. You will need a server and a gateway program. Installing these is a specialised task. If you already have an office server, you could install a mail server program. Each user sends and receives e-mail using (say) Outlook Express, but they are interacting with the server which is actually dialling into the Internet and doing the transfers via the ISP's multi-user account.

Configuring your e-mail

You ISP will tell you the various parameters you need to connect to the mail system. In particular, you will need to know the incoming and outgoing mail boxes, your account name and any password you need to connect.

E-mail client programs

In order to send and access e-mail you need:

~ a dial-up ISP
~ an e-mail account with that ISP or another provider
~ the connection hardware (modem, ISDN router, LAN card etc)
~ dial-up Networking software
~ an e-mail client – Outlook Express, Netscape Mail, Eudora etc.

Composing and sending e-mail

There is no need to be on-line (connected) when you are composing e-mails, nor to send them one at a time. You can:

~ Connect to receive your e-mails, then log off and close your connection, but keep the e-mail client open so you can read messages and compose replies to send later.

~ Forward or reply to any e-mails, or compose new ones. Use the Send Later option to store them until you connect again.

~ Send when you are ready – usually the program can be set to dial up when you send.

Sending an attachment

This can be a Word document, a video clip, sound, an image etc. MIME (Multipurpose Internet Mail Extensions) handles file formats reliably.

Also, e-mail programs which support MIME can read HTML formatting. Your e-mail messages can be constructed like mini-Web pages, with text effects like bold, italic or colour, numbered and bulleted lists, graphics and links. This makes e-mails more eye-catching and likely to be read.

Make sure your e-mail program is set to send and read HTML – in Outlook Express this is in **Tools, Options, Send**. If the recipient's mail or news program does not read HTML, the message appears as plain text with an HTML file attached, which can be opened in a browser. It is worth including a statement in your messages such as 'Contains formatting – ensure your e-mail client can read HTML'.

Signature files

A signature (or sig) file is a short text (or HTML-formatted) file at the foot of every message. This was originally intended as a standard paragraph including the sender's name, address, phone number etc to save typing this every time. But your sig file could carry a promotional message – 'This week only – free widget with every 25 ordered'.*

Don't make it too large – nobody will thank you for making them spend ten minutes of phone bill time downloading something that just goes 'boing'. Make it useful and make it work for you.

If your e-mail can handle formatted text, the Sig lines look like Figure 1.

* Use HTML formatting and you can include coloured text, graphics (such as your logo) or even a piece of music!

Customer Considerations Ltd
e-mail: info@customconsider.com
http://www.customconsider.com/
Tel: 0131-444-3333 Fax: 0131-555-6666
We Sell Everything Good and Everything We
Sell Is Good
Customer Consideration uses ShopShelf
(*http://www.shopshelf.com/*)

Fig. 1. An e-mail sig file.

Notice the contact information and promotional text for a product or service – including someone else's product.

Some e-mail programs allow multiple signature lines so you have the choice of separate business and personal sigs.

Use signature lines and files when posting messages on discussion forums. Someone might just lift the phone or look at your Web site and buy something.

Finding e-mail addresses

Directories

The only sure way to get an e-mail address is to phone someone and ask them! There are no reliably complete e-mail directories as there are phone books. However, there are directories to which Internet users can choose to post an entry. You can also use these to search for postal addresses and other contact details if they are given. The best known are Switchboard at AltaVista (*http://altavista. switchboard.com/*), People Finder at Yahoo (*http://people.yahoo.com/*) and Bigfoot (*http:// www.bigfoot.com/*). Some of these have a very US-bias but there is usually an international section.

Register with as many directories as you can. Give the fullest details possible – address, phone, fax, URL, description of products or services if allowed. Some are divided into *White Pages* (personal addresses) and *Yellow Pages* (business addresses). Some *Yellow Pages* require a payment for a trade advertisement. It is your decision whether the cost is worth it.

Company domains

Larger companies usually have their own domains and give everyone an individual e-mail address (*jim@mycompany.com* or *b.simpson@ourfirm.co.uk*) so knowing an

employee's name will give you a chance of
knowing the e-mail address.

ISPs

If you know someone is registered with a
given ISP you can usually search for their
name in the ISP's site.

Use your Literature

Put your e-mail address on all your stationery,
business cards, promotional brochures, fliers,
newspaper small ads, a block ad in the local
phone book, posters and shop window.

Mailing groups

As you develop a customer base, collect the
names, addresses, telephone, fax and e-mail
details. This takes discipline!

~ Make it your habit to enter business card
  details daily.

~ Automatically add the address of anyone
  who e-mails you.

~ Regularly put new addresses into Groups.
  In the Outlook Express Address Book, this is
  done using **File, New Group**, or by

double-clicking on an existing Group name. Set up Groups for Customers, Business contacts, Sales etc. You can then send Group e-mails and, at Christmas time, export them to a document to print labels for cards.

~ Integrate your Address Book with other databases. Work out a routine for regularly updating your (shared!) Address Book. Most e-mail address programs have an Import function. If your contact database is in an unrecognised format, export it as a Text file, then import it from that, remembering to match up the field names with the ones in your Address Book.

~ If your computers are on a network then everyone should work from the same Address Book. If you are on free-standing PCs (and laptops) then make it the responsibility of *one* person to collect all new business cards and keep a single version of the Address Book up to date, distributing a new copy weekly for those who also want it on a laptop or at home.

Using mailing lists

The Address Book of your e-mail program is fine for small lists. A postal mail shot to 10,000 potential customers would require you to buy in a mailing list as a database (or a set of labels) or hire a mailing house to do it.

Life is simpler on the Internet. There are more than 40,000 mailing lists available free, not counting newsgroups (see below) although you may not actually see the e-mail addresses. If a list is appropriate to your interest, sector or client group, send an e-mail to it, including your own e-mail address. The message gets sent to everyone on the list and your address is added. Usually you can read previous messages and add comments which are also posted to all members.*

~ Read the mailing list FAQ document. This will explain whether advertising is allowed, product names can be mentioned etc. Break the rules and you will be removed from the list and prevented from posting another message.

~ Some lists allow paid advertising – weigh up the value of this.

* *There is a directory of lists at* http:// www.topica.com/

~ Mailing lists are better for keeping in touch with your peers and business area than for selling or promoting products.

~ You have no control over the quality of the list – generally it will be open to anyone. But you're not paying per item as you would for a mail shot or fax campaign.

Autoreply and forwarding

Autoreply

A customer e-mails you and gets a message back almost instantly, thanking them for being in touch. They might even be fooled into thinking someone reads all e-mails as they arrive. But you're using an Autoresponder. If you are on holiday, ill or abroad, set up a message that says 'Back on the 24th' or something (but more polite and informative) that responds to *all* incoming e-mails.

Perhaps the best time-saver of all is to have your price lists, catalogues etc available as an autoresponder file and to set your e-mail to respond to any e-mail sent to *sales*@.. and with the word 'brochure' or 'price list' in the subject line with an instant piece of literature, plus a link to the URL where you have your full-colour catalogue. Now that's service!

Set up a Message Rule in Outlook Express (in **Tools, Message Rules, Mail**) which responds to any e-mail sent to *support*@... with a simple Thank You message. This can be written using Notepad and saved as thankyou.eml.

There is a way to make e-mail links in Web pages send a subject line.*

Forward e-mails when away from home

ISPs tend to operate in one country – you dial a UK-only 0845 number, for instance. So how do you collect e-mails when abroad? There are three main ways:

1   Establish a new e-mail account (costs money!) with an ISP with a Point of Presence in any country you visit, such as AOL. Forward all your 'real' e-mails to that address and dial in from your laptop.
2   Establish a Web-based 'e-mail address for life' with Yahoo, Netscape or a free ISP

* *If your e-mail link is **mailto:jim@ jim.co.uk? subject "sales"** it will insert the subject "sales" in every e-mail. Different pages could have different subjects.*

and forward all your 'real' e-mails to that. Web-based e-mail can be accessed through a browser, so you will still need some way of getting onto the Internet, such as an Internet café, the hotel computer or your laptop. Your ISP may offer a service whereby your normal e-mail can be read with a browser – ask.

3   Set up an e-mail-to-fax or e-mail-to-phone service for the period you are abroad. Examples of such services can be found at *http://www.j2.com/*.

Alternatively, if the need is great and you can afford it, investigate Microsoft's Outlook Web Access, which allows Web-based reading of standard e-mails, provided Outlook is your basic messaging system.

Can't be bothered?

If you don't fancy the thought of all that autoresponding set up, your ISP may do it for you. Or, if your company runs a network, get the network manager to organise an automated mailbot listserver routine.*

* *A 'robot' (a program) which automatically delivers information via e-mail, such as a message to everyone in a database.*

Netiquette

Internet (and especially e-mail) is a superb way to reach a lot of people quickly and cheaply. But abuse it – sending blatant adverts, becoming an e-mail pest, badgering potential customers, sending spam to everyone in your Address Book – and you will get named, blamed and flamed. You will be unable to join mailing lists or subscribe to newsgroups.*

Some basic rules:

1   Consider carefully what you write since it might be forwarded to others.
2   Read your e-mail before you send it.
3   Don't attach large files (over 50K) without permission from the recipient.
4   Never attach files when posting to discussion groups.
5   Never send Web pages to a discussion group, even though most browsers have an in-built facility to do just that. Send the URL as a link and why you think it interesting.
6   Don't promote your business too obviously – like posting an advert to a

* If someone complains to your ISP they may revoke your e-mail account or Web site.

discussion group – unless it is an accepted practice and/or you have checked first.

7   Don't quote back an entire message when responding – just the bit you are responding to. Put your comments at the top of the message rather than the bottom.

8   DON'T TYPE IN ALL CAPS. This is shouting.

9   e-mail may be cheap to some, but not to everyone, so be succinct.

10 Don't use cutesy acronyms like IMHO (in my humble opinion) or BTW (by the way).

11 Make your Subject line interesting, descriptive and meaningful. Busy people only open messages which appeal to them at first glance.

12 Never forward personal e-mails to a discussion group or another party without the author's permission.

13 Turn off e-mail formatting when posting to a discussion group – a lot of programs can't handle it – and limit lines to 65-70 characters.

Organise your e-mail for marketing

Setting up a Web site is covered on pages 61

– 76, but e-mail plays a valuable role in promoting that site, and as a marketing tool in its own right.

Push e-mail

E-mail is an example of 'push' technology – you send it out *to* people rather than wait for them to find it. What will get people to it.

1   Establish a regular newsletter by e-mail and invite people to subscribe. You are then justified in e-mailing them. Make it easy to unsubscribe.
2   Make your newsletter different from others. Think up something you as a customer would like to know – even industry jokes.
3   If you update your site regularly (which you must) send a weekly or monthly e-mail to say so. Make sure a visitor can request this.
4   If you do send a bulk e-mail, put *all* the recipients in the BCC (Blind Carbon Copy) field, otherwise everyone will know everyone else's e-mail address. There are many mailing list services, including

Yahoo eGroups (*http://groups.yahoo.com/*) and Topica (*http://www.topica.com/*) – both free, but they insert their own advertising – and BusinessMail (*http://www.businessemail.com*).

5   ISSN numbers lend credibility. Register an e-mail newsletter or e-zine with the US Library of Congress (*http://lcWeb.loc.gov/issn/e-serials.html*). This may get your publication onto a few more lists.

6   Promote your newsletter in mailing lists and newsgroups (if allowed). Make it a valuable service to interested people.

7   Give away free information. Make people visit your Web site to get it.

8   Consider different language versions – potential customers may not be getting any information from your competitors, because they can't translate it. Find a student from the relevant country.

9   There are automated translation services, like AltaVista's Babelfish (*http://uk.altavista.com/trns)*.

10 If there's a newsletter you particularly like or find useful, offer to translate it in exchange for an advert, a link to your site etc.

11 Apart from mailing lists and newsgroups there are bulletin boards, Web site discussion pages and forums. If someone wants to know more about what you sell, suggest gently that there is free information on your Web site. (Make sure there is!)

12 If you sell software, get into discussion groups and suggest that you solved that problem, will send a demo, see my Web site etc.

13 Get into e-zines. They may charge for an advert, but for free they may review your book, list your Web site if it offers something new or different or accept a submission on a relevant subject. Slip in a reference to your site.*

14 Start your own newsgroup. Just as there are 40,000 mailing lists, there are 40,000 newsgroups. Look at Google's Deja News (*http://www.dejanews.com*) for a near-complete listing. If your idea is good enough you may persuade your ISP to set it up and maintain it.

15 When posting to a newsgroup, include a sig file with a link to your URL (see p 46) just as you would with an e-mail.

* *There is a slightly outdated list of e-zines at* http://www.meer.net/~johnl/e-zine-list/ *and you can submit articles using automated submission (page 128).*

Using correct English

Do not ignore the basic rules of spelling, punctuation, syntax and grammar. My own six *bêtes noirs* are:

~ The plural of MOT is MOTs, not MOT's and PC's means 'of the PC'. However, 'It's' means 'It is' and 'Its' means 'belonging to it'. 'Who's' is short for 'who is' and 'whose' means 'belonging to whom'.

~ Avoid exclamations (!) except for real emphasis (FREE!).

~ A preposition (like 'with') is a bad thing to end a sentence *with*.

~ *And* never start a sentence with a conjunction, like 'And'.

~ If you write something clumsy, there is another way to express it.

~ Spell-checkers *can't* distinguish between correctly-spelt but wrongly-used alternatives (like '*can't*' and '*cant*').

5 Essential Web Site

If you have an existing Web site, this section may contains ideas and concepts which your current site does not incorporate.

When you connect to the Internet for Web or e-mail, you are using a **dial-up** to an Internet Service Provider (ISP) who provides a **host** service on a **server** (the physical computer where your Web site, e-mail, post-boxes etc are). When you connect to e-mail, any new messages are downloaded to your **e-mail client** (the program you use to access e-mail) on your **client PC** (the one on your desk). When you access any Web site, whatever its **domain** (the name it is known by, like *microsoft.com* or *fifeweb.net*), your **browser** (the program which displays Web pages, like Netscape or Internet Explorer) temporarily downloads these pages so you can view them. If you have your own Web site, you will **upload** it to the **host**, probably using File Transfer Protocol (FTP, see p 30**)** so it resides on the server, where everyone can view it.

Building your own Web site

There are many advantages to building a Web site from scratch.

~ You determine and control its appearance – this may not be possible if your Web space comes as part of a 'free' package.

~ You can add interactive elements and e-commerce (which some Web site hosts don't allow – including the 'free' ISPs associated).

~ You can integrate on-line catalogues and shopping cart systems from the outset rather than later.

~ You can choose interesting effects and technologies (animation, shockwave, audio, video etc).

~ You can build in discussion forums, on-line customer support.

~ You can control your own domain – move it to another server if you get a better deal, add to it, update it regularly and so on.

The disadvantages are:
~ You have to do it yourself, or get someone

else to do it for you.

~ You, or your Web designer, is going to have to invest in the e-commerce software – an extra expense.

~ You have to keep the catalogue, price list etc up to date.

~ You have to do stock control, order processing, posting or dispatching the orders.

If you have an existing Web site you can have a second, custom-built site elsewhere with links between them.*

Web site hints

Your Web site is a shop window to millions of potential customers, but:

~ they won't all see it

~ of those who do, a small percentage will interact with it

~ of those, a minuscule number will buy anything.

However, if everyone you sell to comes back

* *This book does not deal with Web site creation – consult* Creating a Web Site *by Bruce Durie (How To Books).*

for another purchase or more information, you have the beginnings of a loyal customer base. Therefore your Web site should be: .

~ well-known
~ attractive
~ easy to interact with
~ constantly offering something new
~ 'sticky' – people stay and come back.

With 350 million Web pages to look at, who's going to look at yours? Nobody, if they don't know it exists. And they won't stay if they don't like it. Here are five hints to help solve these problems.

Hint 1: speed

Site speed is the time (in seconds) needed for a user to download and view your start page at 28.8Kbps using a dial-up connection. Many people use 56K modems, ISDN or leased lines, but a lot don't. Any more than ten seconds and you'll lose them. If your page is slow to load cut down the graphics, clever Java and dynamic HTML effects, or use a gif or jpg optimiser to compress your graphics. Does your gif logo need to be in 16 million colours when 16 might do? Use standard fonts other

browsers will have loaded. Stick to the
Netscape 216 colour palette.

Hint 2: navigation

Site navigation must be easy, logical, intuitive
and consistent. Mouse-overs, rollovers and
image-swapping help if:

~ They don't make the loading time too high.

~ The effect is consistent, not lit up like a
  fairground.

~ There are no broken links, the main turn-
  off for casual browsers – check your links
  often to make sure the sites or pages
  haven't gone away or been moved.

~ The physical structure of the site should
  reflect its organisation – have different
  groups of pages in separate folders
  (Images, Products, Orders, Database, etc).

~ Don't be clever with names – if you have a
  Customer Contact form, call it
  customer_contact.htm, put it in a folder
  called customer_contact and make sure its
  title is Customer Contact.

~ Call your initial page index.htm or

default.htm and make its title Home or *MyCompany* Home.

~ The simplest navigation is the embedded link – for *cheeses*, click *here* (both *cheeses* and *here* link to the same document).

~ Point with pictures – an image is a better way to label a navigation link than a word.

~ However, the reason a picture is worth a thousand words is that there may be a thousand ways to interpret an image without context. Add a text label to make it obvious.

~ Every graphic should have ALT text associated with it – and something meaningful, not just wdfr1462.gif – because:

   (a) when the mouse goes over it, the visitor sees what it's about
   (b) some people will have their graphics turned off.

Hint 3: image is all

This is where a designer can help – someone with an eye for colour, shape and form. Your

Web should reflect the nature, function, purpose and audience of your business. It must also be functional. The most successful sites work well, load fast and have an understated, quality look. Never use more than two type faces on any one page and keep this consistent throughout the site. Use a font size large enough to read but small enough to fit.*

Hint 4: get them in and hang on to them

'Site pull' is your Web's ability to attract visitors and 'stickiness' is a measure of how long they stay and how often they come back. The best attraction is often a forum for visitors to communicate with you and each other.

~ Does your site sell cars? Set up a discussion page on new models or classic marques.

* *Use a bright coloured font against a dark background (or vice-versa) and you can often get away with a smaller size.*

~ Do you deal in comics? Give users (and yourself) a chance to rave about the latest *X-Men*.

~ Lawyer? Provide a message board where clients and other lawyers can swap news about bits of legislation.

Hint 5: push your site

'Site push' technology allows you to 'push' your products or services to your visitors. It works if it isn't too intrusive or unwelcome. The commonest 'push' is a listbot service where you offer visitors a product, service or freebie in return for their e-mail address.*

Add to an existing site

Among the things you can add to a Web site are:

~ electronic shop-front or catalogue
~ payment systems
~ forms for customer data collection
~ chat rooms
~ forums or message board
~ links to other sites
~ additional pages or sub-Webs
~ database integration.

However, check that your ISP and host can handle cgi scripts, FrontPage extensions and other technology you want to use. Your ISP's

* *A listbot is an e-mail based program similar to a mailbot which manages lists of (for example) sales prospects, members of a newsgroup targeted subscribers and is usually capable of generating reports.*

support people will tell you what is possible and may suggest alternatives.

Some ISPs have their own approved cgi scripts, counters, WebStat services, form e-mail programs, e-commerce shopping carts etc.

Register domain name

Your domain name is the heart of your Internet identity and your on-line brand. A domain name is an alias. Computers use Internet Protocol (IP) numbers to locate each other. However 127.123.456.789 is hard to remember and not as user-friendly as *www. widgets.com*. When you type *www.widgets.com* into a Web browser or send e-mail to *fred@widgets.com*, the Domain Name System (DNS) translates this into IP numbers and connects you.

If you know what you want your domain name to be, register it. If you are not ready to go on-line with a Web site, reserve a domain and so protect your Internet brand until it is ready to use.

Domain names disappear fast, either

because someone else has the same idea and gets in first, or because they register it speculatively to sell on later. This is known as 'domain name warehousing' and is increasingly common.

Your ISP or Web host will provide you with the technical information you need when you register your domain, in order to 'point' it at their computers.

Finding out whether your domain name is available

Your ISP or host may have a domain name search service on their main site. Otherwise, use Internic (*http://www.internic.net/* or Nominet (*http://www.nic.uk/*). A search will also tell you who owns, who hosts and who registered the domain. They also maintain a list of Registrars who can register on your behalf. Some of them may have special offers or deals.

Easyspace (*http://www.easyspace.com/*) and UK2 (*http://www.uk2.net*) charge very small amounts – as low as £2 – £5 ($3 – $8). Prices should include InterNIC registration fees and a free email account. *

* Most registration services have an on-line facility, so have a credit card handy – this is an e-Business in its own right.

Your ISP may register your name for you and charge you the appropriate fee. ConnectFree (*http://www.connectfree.co.uk/*) will provide free registration (.co.uk and .org names) for the cost of a three-minute phone call at £1.50 per minute plus £5 every two years. They charge £25 if you then move the domain name to another host.

Some ISPs, especially the free ones, will only give you names that are subdomains of their own (*joanjones.freeserve.co.uk*) and may require you to take advertising.

This is not a recommendation for any of these services. Prices and deals change from time to time, so check. Moving your domain name may not be easy (see p 74).

Choosing your domain name

Letters, numbers and hyphens can be used. You cannot begin or end a domain name with a hyphen – so *my-site.com* is fine, but *-mysite.com* is not. Spaces, apostrophes ('), exclamation marks (!) and underscores (_), are not allowed in Web addresses. However, you can have some special characters in file names – *mysite.com/start_here.htm* would be OK if your server allows it – some do, some don't.

A Web address can be up to 63 characters long including the dot and the three or more characters of top-level domain (.com, .net, .org etc).

The .com, .net, .org, .co.uk and .plc suffixes

~ The *.com*, *.net* and *.org* domain suffixes are not affiliated with any country – anyone from anywhere can register these. A lot of business Web addresses end in .com because this suffix looks smarter and more global than .co.uk.

~ There are 191 country-code top-level domains – like .uk for the UK and .de for Germany (Deutschland). Each country has its own registration requirements – some country codes are restricted and you would have to meet strict local residence, business registration, tax or trademark guidelines. Other country-code domains are unrestricted (like .com). This is the case in over 80 countries – anyone can register your company or brand name in the

country-specific domain. Large companies
spend several thousand pounds on 'global
registration', so the domain is registered in
every possible combination.

~ Domains ending in .co.uk signify a UK-
based company, but there is no necessity
for you to be a registered company or to
be in the UK. It is one of the easiest and
cheapest domain suffixes to get.

~ Domains registered as .plc must be PLCs –
you will have to provide evidence in the
form of a Company Registration Number or
similar documentation.

~ Others such as .edu, .ac. gov and .mil are
reserved for education, academic,
government and US military. Forget it.

http://www

The 'www.' or 'http://www' parts are not part
of your domain name. They are part of
another type of Internet address used on the
Web called a Universal Resource Locator
(URL). There is no real need to have 'www.'
before your domain name to identify your
Web site, but it is typical as it lets people

know it is an actual Web address with content. What you register is the domain (without the *www.* part).

Transferring your domain name

Every Web site must be physically on a host computer. There are also Domain Name Hosts connected to the Internet which translate URLs into IP addresses and direct browsers to your site host. When you register or reserve a domain name, it is recorded on a Domain Name Host.

When you sign up with an Internet Service Provider (ISP) or Web hosting service, or if your organisation has its own host servers, you will upload your Web site to their computers and give them permission to hold your domain name. The Domain Name Host directs any browser to the IP address of that computer.

If you change your ISP or move your Web site to another computer, there is a process for transferring domains between hosts which involves you giving permission for the new host to use the IP 'tag'.

Your existing or new ISP can do this for you, but may charge or may make it difficult.

Your domain name is valuable

You can sell a domain name you own. But if you register domain names for the purpose of selling them on (warehousing), be careful. Recent judgements in the UK and USA say that copyright carries over onto the Internet. For every genius who has made a fortune out of *elvis.com* or *wallstreet.com* there is some other poor soul being dragged through the courts by a large company or a well-known footballer. Someone may choose to make an example of you. To them, it's only money. It could be your house.

Ownership of your domain name

~ Retain any certificates you receive and print any e-mails the Registrar sends you. These may be required if there is ever a dispute over ownership.

~ Make sure you actually own the domain name. Some companies are intermediaries – they own the name but allow you to use it. If it proves to be popular they may ask for a high fee for you to continue.

~ Always pay the annual or two-year registration fee immediately. You should receive e-mail reminders in time. If it lapses, someone may snap it up instantly.*

REGISTRY WHOIS

Whois Server Version 1.3

Domain Name: E-BUSINESS-ESSENTIALS.COM
Registrar: EASYSPACE LTD
Whois Server: whois.easyspace.com
Referral URL: http://www.easyspace.com
Name Server: NS0.FIRSTNET.CO.UK
Name Server: NS3.FIRSTNET.CO.UK
Updated Date: 06-jun-2000

Administrative Contact, Billing Contact, Technical Contact: "Dr Bruce Durie" <domains@convenient-fiction.co.uk>

Last update of whois database: Mon, 28 May 2001 01:56:18 EDT

Note: this information can be 24 hours out of date.

* *There is software which trawls for lapsed and available domain names and instantly bags them.*

Fig. 2. A whois domain listing.

6 Essential Visitors

Attracting visitors to your site

Owning a Web site can feel a bit like owning an ice-cream stall on the moon – nobody comes to it and, if they did, they probably wouldn't buy what you sell. Web sites have to look good, be technically clever and match the owner's objectives.

You also have to build awareness, traffic and 'stickiness'. Unless people know about your site, visit it, stay long enough to part with money and come back again ('stickiness') you may as well be selling lilos in the desert.

~ Put *at least* as much effort into promoting and nurturing your site as into its design and creation.

~ Many good-looking sites fail – they are designed by people who don't give any thought to building an audience or don't know how.

Drive traffic to your site

Obvious but expensive

Take out a newspaper or TV ad if you can afford it.

Use search engines

This is the most important thing you can do with your site. See page 81 for more details.

Make reciprocal links

If you find a site you like and is relevant, put a link to it in your site.*

Then e-mail the people concerned and ask if they will do the same. Think what else your prospective visitors may want that you don't offer, and where else they might be browsing.

~ If they visit a healthfood site, will they buy your organic fruit?

~ If they visit the local theatre site will they buy your prints of early posters?

~ If they enjoy looking at pictures of trains, would they like your information pack on *Getting A Life*?

* *Some search engines rate a site by how many other sites link to it. Have a page of links in your site.*

Web rings

Web sites can be organised into loose confederations of similar-subject 'rings' which may also include advertisers. Check for rings relevant to you at *http://www.webring.org*

Discussion lists, newsgroups and e-zines

These are dealt with in more detail on pages 84 and 122. Being helpful and informative in a discussion will do wonders for your credibility and your traffic.

Traditional marketing

~ Use personal networks.

~ Put your Web site URL and e-mail on stationery and cards.

~ Don't rule out fliers and small ads in the local free papers.

~ If you sell books, put your URL and e-mail on bookmarks.

~ Get on local radio to talk about some other subject, and plug your site mercilessly.

~ Write to the local newspaper about some burning issue – and get your URL in the letter.

~ Give a prize (bottle of wine, box of chocolates, a book) to every hundredth person who visits or takes your e-mail newsletter, and have your URL emblazoned on it.

Site awards

These mean very little – you mostly get them by just asking.

Banner ad programmes

If every banner exchange worked, every site would be full of banner ads and nothing else. Some banner ads can be tied to affiliate programmes which may earn extra income. Once your site is pulling in visitors, you can sell your page space to others. See p 88.

Paid site submission services.

'For a mere £99.99 you can get into the top ten of all the major search engines.' With a few exceptions, these are a scam. If there were any truth to this, every site would be in the top ten. Impossible.

Send on-line press releases

Generate interest in your site by telling thousands of people via on-line press release services.*

Making your Web pages search-engine friendly

~ AltaVista, Yahoo, Lycos, Excite etc are the single major source of traffic and referrals for most Web sites. They are also free.

~ There are automated submission engines and paid submission services. However, you can do it manually.

~ Most search engines and directories have a 'Submit your URL' link somewhere on the main page.

~ Work out a description of your site in 12 words and a longer one (say 50) then write a list of 20 keywords which describe your site and which you think may attract visitors.

* *Free press release services are listed on p 127.*

~ Keep this in a text file so that you can cut and paste.

~ The three most important things are:
1   give each page on your site a detailed and specific title
2   use meta tags
3   submit to the important search engines every month – listed on p 122.

Meta tags

At the top of every Web page there are hidden meta tags which carry information about the page and send keywords and a description to search engines (Fig 3, page 85). Add or alter these by editing your page in HTML (text) form, or your Web design program may let you add them using a dialogue box.

~ To see the meta tags in a Web page, save the page as a text-only file and open it in a text editor such as Notepad. Some HTML editors allow you to view a page as text. Browsers have a **View, Source** option.

~ If you see a site that receives a high ranking view the HTML and simply copy and paste the keyword meta tags, amending them to suit your own page and site (eg add your company name).

~ If you are not comfortable with HTML, there are programs which will generate meta tags for you. One which does this – and also submits your pages to search engines – is WebPosition Gold (*http://www.Webpositiongold.com/*). There is a free trial version.

~ Subscribe to the free *MarketPosition* Newsletter – techniques and tips on improving your search engine rankings.

Other search engine tricks

These tips will help improve your rankings on search engines. Not all work with all engines.

~ Have a meaningful description of your site, products and service etc near the top of your first page (index.htm). Some engines use this to generate their search database entries.

~ Use hidden text – repeat your keywords as 'real' text near the top of your index page, but make the text colour the same as the background. No one will see it except the search engine.

~ Send your URL to Link sites and FFA (Free

For All) sites to improve your 'links'
rankings.

Submitting e-zine articles

There are over 80,000 on-line newsletters and
e-zines. Almost all rely on contributors like
you for articles, advice, tips, good links etc.
Find the most relevant e-zines for your
business and offer them articles. Include your
name, company, e-mail address and Web site
URL.

The sites listed on page 128 will automate
the process – post your article on the site and
set up an autoresponder (page 52) to send
the article by e-mail to anyone who requests
it. Some sites have an announcement service.
Among the best are:

~ e-Zine Articles(*http://www.ezinearticles.com/
  add_url.htm*)
~ Idea Marketers (*http://www.ideamarketers.
  com/*)
~ Web Source (*http://www.Web-source.net/
  articlesub.htm*)

```
<title>Silly Software - best prices on the Web</title>
<head>
<meta name="keywords" content="promotion, software,
marketing, advertising, freeware, shareware, best,
prices, best prices, database, Promotion, Software,
Marketing, Advertising, Freeware, Shareware, Best,
Prices, Best Prices, Database">
<META NAME="DESCRIPTION" CONTENT=" Silly Software -
best prices on the Web for freeware, shareware and
downloads. Database software a speciality.">
</head>
```

Fig 3. Meta tags with keywords and description

Tracking your visitors

What you want to know:

~ Who are your visitors?
~ What do they like when they visit?
~ What do they do when they visit?
~ What page do they visit most or stay at for longest?
~ Where they came from (called the 'referrer' site).

This information is essential for:

~ your own marketing (so you can target

high-potential customers and those who don't buy anything)
~ site improvements
~ selling space to advertisers
~ knowing which links, banner ad campaigns etc are working.

Traditional methods

You could track customer responses by phone or postal surveys. This is expensive, slow and unreliable.*

Web methods

Customers needn't know they are being tracked. Each time someone loads a page, clicks on a thumbnail graphic, downloads a file, video clip or audio track, accesses a database or fills in a form, a request goes to the host computer to send information and commands to the visitor's computer. The host computer can log all of this if set up to do so. The data are saved in log files which can be viewed, saved or printed out. Usually some logging software is available on the server. If not, free software is available to do this. Some tracking reports are in database format

* There are straightforward ways to gather this information on the Web.

software, so they can be analysed easily.

There is also hit-rate tracking software which gives more detailed information – what browser a visitor uses, what site the visitor came from, at what modem speed and via what type of Internet access account (.com, .gov, .org etc), error messages which tell you that at certain times the site gets overloaded or the server can't cope etc.

Hits are not visitors

Why do you need that when your site has a counter? A "hit" is counted each time a visitor clicks on part of the site, and for each graphic or link on a page. Loading a page with five graphics on it registers as six hits. So those 1,000 hits a week your counter registers may really only be 30 or 40 visitors.

Starting with a free service

Many companies will give you a free hit counter, tracking software, reporting system and other analysis tools. They may sell this information to other Internet marketing agencies or use it themselves.

~ Hitometer (*http://Websitegarage.netscape. com/*). The free version has a choice of counters and limited on-line and e-mail reporting. Paste a few lines of HTML into your page.

~ Web-Stat (*http://www.Webstat.com/*) has a free 30-day demo and a full registered version at £3 (about $5) per month.

Exchange programmes

LinkExchange (*http://www.linkexchange.com*) is the best known. The banners are big (440x40). Category selection is possible. Hyperbanner Network (*http://www. hyperbanner.net*) is without category selection and with bigger banners (468x60). It can be made country specific – target countries with a language specific page.

Info-Links Index (save a blank e-mail to *adinfo@info-links.com*) is not an exchange program as such. It costs about £7 ($10) per 1000 'impressions'.

TrafficX (*http://www.TrafficX.com/*) 'guarantees' one visitor per two people who click on banners and ten guarantees for every person you introduce to the programme. Full-sized (400x40, 468x60) and microbanners (88x31) can be placed almost anywhere.

Using forms

Web site forms

The information you really want (names and e-mail addresses) is anonymous unless provided voluntarily. The best way to get this is by asking visitors to complete a form. Most modern Web design packages produce forms which send the information to you by e-mail or write it to a database. As well as 'who are you' information you might ask for:

~ income level
~ interests
~ number of family members
~ recent purchases
~ where they live.

Registration forms

Some sites require visitors to register before they can get beyond an introductory page. The registration form is typically short and asks for general information, possibly name and e-mail address. Visitors get a confirmation and a password by e-mail to access the site.

It doesn't always work. Lots of Web visitors dislike being tracked and will avoid sites that do so. They also provide false information, false e-mail addresses and give out the passwords to others.*

Tracking information can also have an immediate impact. If you enter a keyword in AltaVista you will probably see a banner ad linked to your search. If you had a property-letting site and someone searched for houses in say Carlisle, the tracking software could fill the site with links to car rental agencies, visitor attractions within 10 miles and so on. Other companies will pay well if you convince them their information is getting to targeted groups.

Use both

~ Find a Web counter or stats service which tells you what you want to know (try a few or more than one at a time – they can be hidden so no one realises).

* To get the most accurate results keep the form short, simple and non-intrusive.

~ Design your own form to collect the more detailed information on individual visitors.

7 Essential Web Site Improvements

Supercharge your Web site

Your Web site is there and it works. But:

~ Could it work better?
~ Could it have more components and functionality?
~ Could it be more of an asset to your business?

Of course it could.

Web databases

~ Make your Web site attractive by providing information visitors would find it hard or inconvenient to get themselves.
~ Make it interactive.
~ Keep it fresh with new, relevant information.

You can do all three by using a Web database. Examples would be:

~ A list of upcoming events and exhibitions.
~ Latest information on spare parts.

~ A list of e-mail addresses and phone numbers of suppliers.

You would probably find these useful yourself. Running an e-Business means getting as much information as possible into computerised form and using it to its best advantage. If others found it useful, it would drive visitors to your site.*

If your business is database-driven – like an advertising magazine, an estate agent or an insurance broker – then give users access to it via the Web. Exchange and Mart (*http://www.ixm.co.uk/*) is one big database, updated when someone phones or sends in an advertisement. Another example is Booksearch UK (*http://www.booksearchuk.co.uk/*).

Databases collect information

You can also store the results of forms in a database. If you were collecting names of club members, they could input their details directly and other users could access the list (if allowed by you).

* *This is the thinking behind the Local Hotel Web databases run by Tourist Boards and the whole concept behind Amazon.*

Getting your database on-line

This is not as straightforward as simple Web page design. If you are a very small business with your site hosted elsewhere, it can be frustrating. You will need either a CGI script to search the database or to construct your site using FrontPage, which has basic but robust data handling tools. Neither is a job for an amateur.

CGI scripts

A CGI (Common Gateway Interface) script is an executable program, usually written in language like Perl. Check whether your ISP allows CGI scripts to be run. Then check whether they have a library of CGI scripts available, including a database search script. If so, get as much detail as you can on how it works and what you need to do. Even if you do not write your own CGI scripts you will have to put the 'queries' (the commands which tell the script which database to search and for what) into your Web pages. For on-line script archives and tutorials, Matt's Script Archive (*http://scriptarchive.com/*) and CGI Resources (*http://www.cgi-resources.com/*) are a good starting point.

FrontPage

Microsoft's Web page design tool is fast
becoming a favourite for constructing sites. It
uses ASP (Active Server Page) technology to
provide database access without CGI
programming. An associated product,
VisualStudio, has a range of development
tools to help further. To run a FrontPage Web
your server must have FrontPage extensions
(additional files) installed. Not all ISPs operate
FrontPage servers and those that do may
charge extra. If you go down this route, take
the opportunity to use FrontPage to its fullest
extent and get a jazzed-up Web site out of it.
The FrontPage 2000 45-day demo is available
from Microsoft (*http://www.microsoft.com.uk/*).

FrontPage Express

Microsoft's simple (and free) Web page design
tool has the capability to build in a Search
Form, which searches for text in your site. FP
Express should have come with your Internet
Explorer. If not, upgrade to IE5 or download
FP Express separately from Microsoft. It is also

available on various PC magazine CDs.

Keep it simple

If all you want to do is provide information on 30 upcoming events, 40 suppliers' addresses or a catalogue of 50 items, it may be simpler to have these as 30, 40 or 50 individual Web pages accessible from hyperlinks in a Web page made to look like a database. You will have to change the information pages and the text in the links as the data change, which can be time-consuming.

Alternatively, use FrontPage Express to create a page containing a WebBot (a piece of built-in programming) which searches for text in Web pages. Put all your informational pages in a new folder and direct the form to search in that folder only instead of 'All'.

Web telephones

The Internet uses the phone lines to send data to and from anywhere in the world, for the price of a local phone call. So why not use it for phone calls to anywhere in the world? If your computer has a sound card, speakers and a microphone, all you need is some specialised software to make Internet phone calls. If you have Netscape Navigator 3 or above, you may have the appropriate software. Some modems also bundle it with their installation programs. Properly installed, some of these allow visitors to your site to contact you directly by voice. NetVoice (*http://www.netvoice.com*), Net2Phone (*http://www.net2phone.com/*) and Firetalk (*http://www.fivetalk.com/*) are worth investigating. Invest in a headset to improve quality and leave both hands free.

These programmes may require you to buy 'phone time'.

8 Essential Selling On-line

Advantages of an on-line shop:

~ Open 24 hours a day, 7 days a week ('24/7' service).

~ No staff costs, rent, utility bills or other overheads, other than your time and phone bills.

~ No stock requirement (if you are not selling physical goods).

~ Good cash flow (you get the money first).

~ Customers can be tracked.

~ Global reach.

~ The on-line shop.

The basic components of an on-line shop are:

~ A Web site showing or describing your products or services.

~ A payment system.

~ One or more databases for stock, customer details and orders.

~ A delivery system.

Getting your shop

Time to set yourself up for credit card payments over the Internet. You have three basic options:

1.   join an e-mall (page 99)*
2.   use a site shop builder or turnkey solution (page 100)
3.   do it yourself (page 101).

In general the best advice is:

~ *Small number of items, small number of transactions*: sign up with shop.yahoo.com, Amazon's z-Shops etc (page 100).

~ *Small number of items, large number of transactions*: design your own site using a shop creation program and host it under your own domain name. Invest in Merchant software to handle your own order processing (or use your ISP's) but don't pay a charge-per-item or percentage.

~ *Large number of items, large number of transactions*: negotiate with your ISP to set up secure site with shopping cart, payment system, own merchant account etc and have a professional site make-over.

*   *A shopping mall developer will rent you shop space and look after things like cleaning, lighting and security. An e-mall owner will provide you with Web space, a shop front and all the 'back-office' functions.*

~ *Large number of items, small number of transactions:* if each transaction is for a reasonable amount (computers, cars, yachts, houses or expensive software), use a third-party Merchant Service which charges per month, not a percentage of each transaction or the total. Otherwise, process orders manually by e-mail.

Joining an e-mall

The first major example of e-malls was Barclay Square (*http://www.barclaysquare.co.uk/*). They have pros and cons:

Plus	Minus
~ Easy to set up the site	~ Little control over site design.
~ Exclusive in whom they allow to join	~ May be too exclusive.
~ Specific to one locality or business sector.	~ They may be too specific, or not specific enough.
~ Few hidden costs.	~ Can be expensive.
~ Handle all transactions.	~ May not pay quickly.
~ Lots of publicity, exposure and visitors (if it's a good one).	~ No control over attracting visitors.

See also Amazon's z-Shops (*http://www. amazon.co.uk*) and shop.yahoo (*http://shop. yahoo.com/*).

Site shops and turnkey solutions

This is a slightly different idea along the same lines – a company provides you with a Web template (so you don't have to do any design) and all the transactional, site submission and visitor tracking tools, then hosts your site for you. Netscape has a basic example (*http://smallbusiness.netscape.com/ smallbusiness/main.tmpl*).

There are more controllable systems (you have some hand in the design and you appear to be independent). IBM's HomePage Creator (*http://www.ibm.com/businesscentre/ uk/*) is a well known example as is Electrom (*http://www.electrom.com/*) which is specialised for FrontPage users (see p 94).

Pros	Cons
˜ Easy to set up the site.	˜ All sites look the same.
˜ May allow you to design a site 'off' their standard	˜ May not allow certain programming

templates and upload it.

~ Single, monthly or annual charge.

~ Low 'basic' cost.
~ Handle all transactions.
~ You can control and dictate visitor targeting and tracking.

techniques (frames, CGI etc).

~ Often a confusing set of payment options.

~ Charges can spiral.
~ May not pay promptly.
~ It may get very lonely if no one comes.

Shop creation programs

Most storefront, shopbuilder or shopping cart software operates the same way:

~ Enter your information (name, phone, fax, address, e-mail etc).
~ Design the store using standard templates.
~ Add in graphics, multimedia etc.
~ Add product information.
~ Choose options (tax, shipping, discount, foreign currency, secure transaction processing).
~ Save and upload to your ISP.

Typically they come with style templates

(usually frames) and a choice of tax, shipping, discount, foreign currency, secure transaction processing systems and other options.

You do not need to be connected to the Internet to create your shop. The generated Web pages are uploaded to your Web site by FTP (page 30). Usually there is no need to know HTML or CGI programming, although this would help with customisation.

Sometimes the software comes as part of a paid-for ISP secure server hosting package, but there are stand-alone packages available. These mostly work in the same way.

~ The cheaper ones tend to be very suitable for catalogue-based business (small number of items which do not change much) but they can be inflexible.

~ They generate 'static' pages (eg you can't change a product's details by just changing a database entry).

~ When you add or change a product all the pages are regenerated by the software, obliterating any customisation.

~ They may be difficult to adapt to match your site.

Actinic Catalog (*http://www.actinic.co.uk*), ShopCreator (*http://www.shopcreator.com*) and ShopFactory (*http://www.shopfactory.com*) are low-end solutions for small- to medium-sized businesses wanting a catalogue on the Internet. They lack the advanced tools to generate and maintain a large e-commerce site, but both create a catalogue, generate the Web site, take orders and process them. Free downloadable demos are available to try.

True database-driven, fully customisable shop creation programs are more expensive (see reviews at *http://ecommerce.internet. com/reviews/glance/0,,3691_3,00.html*).*

Catalogue and payment systems

Consider:

~ Do you need multiple catalogue pages or just one? A large page will be slow to load.

~ Do you need different 'departments'?

~ What price are your goods or services? The charges associated with on-line credit card transactions may make small payments uneconomic. Keep credit card sales for

* *A list of Merchant Account Providers with 'turnkey solutions' is given at* http://www. merchantworkz. com/turnkey.asp, *with example rates.*

items costing over, say, £10. There are micropayment systems available for smaller sums (see page 106).

~ Do you want to offer a cheque payment facility? If someone wishes to pay by cheque, have a page which can be printed out as an order form to send along with payment. Set up a FREEPOST address to make it painless but add the cost to the post and packing charge.

~ Will you be taking orders from abroad? There may be a handling or conversion charge. Make sure you can accept Euros.

~ Credit card payments from abroad aren't so much of a problem since they get converted automatically.

~ Don't make your customer leave and re-enter your on-line shop to choose more than one item.

~ How will you price the post and packing? Customers should know it up front. Options are to charge by weight or per unit. If you are selling things which weigh the same, you can add a per-item cost which is known. If they vary in weight, the shipping cost will have to be determined separately.

~ You can also offer a choice of mailing methods – first and second class, surface or airmail, parcel post or courier. Any decent e-commerce package will have these options built in, but you have to enter the costs.

~ VAT is an issue. Do you know which of your goods attract VAT and at which rate? Find out before you sell them. Even if you are not registered for VAT you still have to charge it.

~ Do you actually have to carry stock? Do a deal with your suppliers – you receive the initial order and eventual payment and send them the orders to fulfil, they do the packing and postage. You have to be able to trust them, because dissatisfied customers are going to come back to you as the merchant, not your suppliers.

~ Can you offer other products alongside your own? If you sell pot plants, establish a link with Amazon so that customers can get gardening books. You will receive a small commission and will never have to pack and post the books.*

Credit card payments

There are three basic ways to organise this.

1   If you are already a merchant (ie can take physical credit cards) your card company or bank may allow you to set up on-line. Ask.

2   There are payment companies which will do it for you. NetBanx is one example. This may well be included with an e-commerce solution such as ShopFactory or Shop@ssistant.

3   If you are reselling someone else's goods (such as books via Amazon or CDs via CDNow) they will handle all payments and send you commission (see p 100).

Merchant services

If you already accept credit cards you have a merchant account. You can extend this to an on-line merchant account. Ask your existing bank or card service provider for details, or

*   *Money for nothing! There are 'reseller' options, link exchanges and banner deals which will net you trouble-free extra income (see p 110).*

use one of the reliable third parties (NetBanx, VeriSign, most of the others listed above or even your own ISP).

Third party banking

All transactions are handled by an intermediary, who may charge commission per sale or a standard charge per transaction, per month or per year. Calculate which is the better deal for you, but bear in mind:

~ There may be a minimum charge regardless of the number of sales (even if none).

~ If you are bringing in £1 million a month and paying the standard £19.99, the company concerned will soon shift you to the percentage-of-value model.

~ Check how and when you can cancel the arrangement – try not to get locked in for a year or have to pay a high penalty to cancel.

An example of the first is NetBanx (*http://www.netbanx.com/*) which will process all transactions and send you the income less any charges. IBM's HomeSite Creator and

Electrom (see page 100) provide transaction processing as part of the standard charge. JustAdd Commerce (*http://www. richmediatech.com*) adds back-office processing to a FrontPage site. In both cases, the site can be hosted anywhere and the product details, ordering forms etc are part of that, but the actual ordering and payment take place on the software company's secure server. Most stand-alone shop creation programs (see page 101) have a similar facility.

A list of merchant account providers with 'turnkey solutions' is at *http://www. merchantworkz.com/turnkey.asp*, with example rates.

Using encryption schemes for secure transactions

If you want to organise your own credit card transactions, you will need a secure Web site. Even if someone else is processing transactions for you it may still be a good idea – especially if people are sending you secure information by e-mail after filling in forms.

The commonest encryption technologies are Secure Sockets Layer (SSL), Secure HTTP (S-HTTP) and (developed for e-mail) PGP.

SSL

This was developed by Netscape and both Netscape, and Internet Explorer browsers can handle it. Check that your ISP supports SSL. The URL may start with https:// instead of the normal http:// and there will be a padlock or a key at the bottom of your browser window. Your server needs to have a 'digital certificate' issued by Verisign (*http://www.verisign.com/*) or another Certification Authority. There is more information at *http://www.microsoft. com/windows/oe/certpage.asp*.

S-HTTP

This is very similar to SSL and is free (*http:// www.nsca.org/*) but is not so widely supported as the proprietary SSL. Both Netscape and Internet Explorer will support it soon and both browsers will be able to connect to S-HTTP or SSL servers.

Encryption for e-mail

Most modern e-mail programs can send and
receive encrypted e-mail. In Outlook Express
set this up using **Tools, Options, Security**
from where you can connect to a site (*http://
www.microsoft.com/windows/oe/certpage.asp*)
that lists Certification Authorities.*

Selling others' products

If all you want to do is sell other people's
software, hardware, information, books, CDs
or other products related to your business or
interest, you can become an Affiliate,
Associate or Reseller (the terms vary). For
instance, you can buy this book via a link
from my site straight to Amazon who will do
everything including posting you the book
and send me a percentage as a commission.
This method can be additional to any
individual payment system you set up for
your own products.

** There is another
security issue –
protecting your
Web site files from
download. This is
dealt with on
p 117.*

Finding new customers

Your Web site is up. You have something to

sell. You know who is visiting and whether and what they buy. You have a subscribers to your free e-mail newsletter. What you need now is an expanding customer base.

Your best new customers are your best existing customers:

~ It costs ten times as much to attract a new customer as to keep an existing one.

~ Don't ignore the ones who have bought from you in the past.

~ Aim for at least 30% of your traffic to be return visitors.

How to build loyalty and return visits

1   Reward loyalty: give discounts for repeat purchases and send a 'thank you' e-mail after three, five or ten responses.

2   Build a sense of belonging to a community: a discussion forum or bulletin board encourages returns. Add a chat room (in a high-traffic site). Advertise specific times when you, at least will be there and be on-line to your chat room at the same time as you upload, download, submit to search engines or

check your e-mail.

3   Hold a weekly or monthly contest: offer a prize for the best, relevant picture or joke. If you have favourite freeware or shareware (and if you are sure it can be distributed) compile it onto a CD and send it to competition winners. Alternatively, buy in CD software collections (around £10) as prizes.

4   Make your pages fresh and update them frequently. A 'What's New' page makes the site look lively.

5   Don't add a counter until your site is a success. If you must, start it at a high but not boastful number like 13254. No one believes them anyway, But 'You are visitor number 0003' is a turn-off.

6   Your newsletter or mailing list should contain free offers.

7   Ask your visitors to put a link in their Web site to yours. Have a special 'link to this site' page with your images, logos and hyperlinks. Make it as easy as possible to copy them. Type 'link:yoursite. co.uk' in the Search box of almost any

search engine to see which sites link to yours. Trade links with other Web sites that have a similar amount of traffic.

8   Think about the sites you visit most often, and why. Be open to new ideas and trial and error.*

Checklist

If you have a biggish site or business:

~ register a domain
~ get SSL from your ISP
~ get a Certificate from VeriSign (needs company documents)
~ get a merchant account or contact card clearing company
~ get a Shopping Cart program
~ design and upload your site.

If you have a smaller site or business:

~ register a domain
~ join a shopfront system from a provider
~ use site tools to produce site
~ link to affiliate programs etc
~ link to your main (home) site
~ get orders by encrypted e-mail

* Judicious swiping of other people's good ideas is fine (without breaking copyright laws).

~ fulfil orders at home/work

~ process card payments manually (if you can take credit cards) or pay extra to have your provider process the transactions.

Regular tasks

Daily

1   Answer your e-mail.
2   Do one marketing task – post an article to a bulletin board or bulk e-mail a newsletter.
3   Search for your company name, keywords or related information.

Weekly

1   Add new keywords to your Web site meta tags.
2   Check what tags your competitors use and incorporate them.
3   Add something to your Web site.

Monthly

1   Submit an article to e-zine publishers (see page 128).
2   Submit your Web pages to a new search

engine.
3   Add your e-mail address and contact
     details to a new directory.

Quarterly

1   Set up a new automated marketing tool,
     eg a new autoresponder.
2   Establish a joint venture with someone
     who sells a similar product.
3   Join a new reseller or affiliate
     programme.

Annually

1   Revamp your existing e-Business.
2   Start a new e-Business.*

** Reward yourself –
have a holiday, a
good night out or
a better car.*

Ideas for e-Businesses

Knowing where to start and knowing what to sell

A good way to get ideas for what to sell is to check what does sell – and then either do the same, or something completely different. (In marketing-speak known as 'following the wind' and 'sailing ahead of the wind'). There are pros and cons to each, and you can, of course, do both.

Selling 'nothing'

The easiest thing to sell on the Web is something non-tangible, or which can be easily digitised for transmission – professional services, documents or software for instance.

Providing documents and files by download

~ The simplest way to provide text and pictures is to have it on your site as Web pages and let users browse it on-line. However, you may not want the information to be so readily available. Put the page in a separate folder and password-protect it.

~ Alternatively, put an abstract or extract on your site and have the full version available as a download or to e-mail on request.

~ If your files are huge or if there are lots of them, produce them on a CD.

~ Do not send document files as Word format (or other text format) unless you want the end-user to be able to edit them. Package the file as Adobe Acrobat Portable Document Format (PDF) or as an 'e-book'.

Selling 'something'

The Web does not provide:

~ Immediacy of acquisition (for tangible objects).

~ The essentials of the retail experience – touching, tasting, using the product (except software).

Therefore the Web has to provide other benefits:

~ Comprehensiveness – your site should have

as much information as possible on a wide range of goods and services.

~ Anticipation of desire – buy a book from Amazon and they will contact you frequently with offers of similar books and gifts.

~ Hands-free – order it on the Web and it gets delivered.

~ Accessory details – a Web site can have links to other places – manufacturer's sites, reviews, technical documents.

~ Follow-on service – offer something extra and free as a 'thank you'.

Reselling and affiliate schemes

Amazon, CDNow and others will provide you with a link for your Web site with a 'tag' so the site knows they came from you. You will receive a commission for each customer who bought something. Affiliate programs will account for 10% of the £3.6 billion ($5.8 billion) of public consumer transactions on the Web in 2000 and perhaps 25% of £20 billion ($35 billion) by 2002. Amazon.com Associate's Program had more than 320,000 affiliated Web sites in early 2000.

Tips and Tricks

1   Are all the hits and e-mails generating sales? If not, which are and why? One customer from ten hits is better than no customers from a thousand.

2   Answer e-mails, take part in on-line mailing list and newsgroup discussions, become recognised as an interested, authoritative figure in your community of interest.

3   You'll never get your print catalogue to Sweden, but they may see your Web site and want to do business. Can you handle it?

4   Put a 'Client Links' page in with company names, short descriptions, e-mail addresses and a link to their URL. This builds customer loyalty, new customer trust and your reputation. Ask them first, and also ask for a reciprocal link on their sites.

5   Have a page of the most frequently asked questions (FAQs) from customers and prospective customers, and the answers.

6   Your Web site isn't really about you – it's

about them, the customers. So give them the information and services they need. Forget values statements, company philosophies, missions, visions, strategies, objectives and organisational growth charts.

7   Check your progress – search for your company name in one of the large search engines. The number of other sites linked to you will tell you how well exposed and recognised you are.

8   Look at those pages and sites of relevance to your business for new ideas on style, presentation, tricks, better technology etc.

9   Find sites that interest your typical target customer (by thinking like them) and offer reciprocal linking. Do a few each day.

10   It will take six months before you see much difference in sales from your site – don't lose heart.

11   Promote your Web address and e-mail on all printed material, answerphone message, shop sign and company car.

12   Use the search engines – see page 122 for details.

13 Set some simple and attainable goals and revise constantly.

14 What's your unique selling point (USP)? Be different.

15 Why do they buy? It saves time. Why don't they buy? They can't look at or try out the product first.

16 If you can't afford a tip-top designer or don't have those skills, get a professionally designed template from the Web.

17 Get your own domain name – otherwise the image you give is someone who isn't making enough money to spend £5 a year.

18 Give away free information.

19 People don't buy from Web sites or shops – they buy from other people they trust.

20 The words on your site should be concise, accurate, free of spelling and grammatical howlers and professional.

21 Let your visitors know what you will do and won't do with information they send. TRUSTe (*http://www.etrust.com/wizard/*) has a wizard to construct a privacy statement.

22 Is your credit card ordering secure? If it

is, say so.

23   Sell one thing – well.

24   Develop an e-mail list – offer a free e-newsletter, discounts, news, hints and tips or something else free and valuable to get e-mails.

25   Contact your e-mail list regularly.

Directories and search engines

There are expanded versions of these lists at *http://www.e-business-essentials.com/ essentials/documents/lists*.htm

Essential search engines

AltaVista *http://www.altavista.com*
Ask Jeeves *http://www.askjeeves.com*
Direct Hit *http://www.directhit.com*
Dmoz *http://www.dmoz.org*
Excite *http://www.excite.com*
Go *http://www.go.com*
Google *http://www.google.com*
Hotbot *http://www.hotbot.com*
Iwon *http://www.iwon.com*
Looksmart *http://www.looksmart.com*

Lycos *http://www.lycos.com*
Microsoft Network *http://www.msn.com*
Netscape *http://www.netscape.com*
Northern Light *http://www.northernlight.com*
Snap *http://www.snap.com*
Webcrawler *http://www.Webcrawler.com*
Yahoo *http://www.yahoo.com*

Essential list directories and search engines

CataList *http://www.lsoft.com/lists/listref.html*
List of Lists *http://catalog.com/vivian/interest-group-search.html*
Liszt *http://www.liszt.com/*
Prodigy Mailing Lists *http://www.goodstuff.prodigy.com/Lists/*
Publicly Accessible Mailing Lists *http://www.neosoft.com/cgi-bin/paml_search/*
TILE.NET *http://www.tile.net/tile/listserv/*
Topica *http://www.topica.com*
Reference.Com *http://www.reference.com/*

Essential promotion

Submit your list to List Directories in addition

to the sites below.

Discussion and List Promotion *http://jlunz.*
databack.com/listpromo.htm
EzineCenter *http://ezinecenter.com/*
FreeShop *http://demo.freeshop.com/corp/*
emailnewsletter.htm
Publishing and Promoting *http://www.*
trafficplan.com/newsltrtips.htm
The List Exchange *http://www.listex.com/*
Hypatia *listserv@hypatia.cs.wisc.edu*

Essential collections of mailing lists

AudetteMedia *http://www.audettemedia.com/*
BulletMail *http://www.bulletmail.com/*
E-Mail Topics *http://www.emailtopics.com/*
Internet/
ListTool.com *http://www.listtool.com/*
Lsoft International *http://www.lsoft.com/*
Mailbase *http://www.mailbase.ac.uk/*
MouseTracks *http://nsns.com/MouseTracks/*
tloml.html

Essential list user resources

Cyber Teddy Online Guide *http://www.*

Webcom.com/teddy/listserv.html

Mailing List Manager Commands *http:// lawwww.cwru.edu/cwrulaw/faculty/milles/ mailser.html*

IFLA's Internet Mailing Lists Guides and Resources *http://www.ifla.org/I/training/ listserv/lists.htm*

E-Mail Discussion Groups *http://alabanza.com/ kabacoff/Inter-Links/listserv.html*

International Business Resources *http://ciber. bus.msu.edu/busres/maillist.htm*

Essential hosting services and list tools

binMail *http://www.binmail.com/binmail*

Coollist *http://www.coollist.com/*

Cuenet Systems *http://www.cuenet.com/*

eGroups.com *http://www.egroups.com/index. html*

E-Mail Publishing, Inc. *http://www.emailpub. com/*

Esosoft's Mailing List *http://www.esosoft.com/ mailinglist/*

ListBot *http://www.ListBot.com/*

Essential software to host discussion groups

Groupmaster *http://www.groupmaster.com*
ListStar *http://www.starnine.com/liststar/
    liststar.html*
L-Soft ListServ *http://www.lsoft.com/*
LWGATE *http://www.netspace.org/users/dwb/
    lwgate.html*
Lyris List Server *http://www.lyris.com/*

Essential list management tips

Turbocheck – send a blank message and
    receive information by e-mail
    *mtotd44@turbocheck.com and
    mailto:mtotd47@turbocheck.com*
Effective Management of Discussion List and
    other e-Mail *http://
    www.Internetadvertising.
    org/resources/emailmanagement.html*
E-mail Publishing Resource Center *http://
    www.emailpub.com/Resource_Main.htm*
E-Publisher Digest *http://www.mmgco.com/
    e-pub/*
The Emailian Newsletter *http://www.emailpub.
    com/Resource_Emailian.htm*

Essential on-line press release services

Comitatus *http://www.comitatusgroup.com/pr/
    index.htm*
M2 PressWire *http://www.m2.com/M2_Press
    WIRE/index.html*
PRWeb *http://www.PRWeb.com*
Webaware *http://www.Webaware.co.uk/netset/
    text/*

Essential message and bulletin boards

Forums List Universe *http://forums.list-
    universe.com/*
Homebusiness *http://homebusiness-Websites.
    com/cgi-bin/index.cgi*
E-zineseek *http://www.ezineseek.com/forum/
    index.cgi*
Free Publicity *http://www.free-publicity.com/
    cgi-bin/talk.cgi*
Her Computer *http://www.hercomputer.com/
    board/index.cgi*
Profitalk *http://www.profitalk.com/*
The Illuminati *http://www.the-illuminati.com/
    board/index.cgi*
WilsonWeb *http://www.wilsonWeb.com/forum/*

Essential e-zines

These sites will take e-zine articles and submit them for you.

Articles *http://216.147.104.180/articles/ submit.shtml*

e-Zine Articles *http://www.ezinearticles.com/ add_url.htm*

E-ZineZ Digest *http://www.e-zines.com/ publishers.htm*

Idea Marketers *http://www.ideamarketers.com/*

Web Source *http://www.Web-source.net/ articlesub.htm*

Writer and Publisher Connection Send a blank e-mail to *article_announce-subscribe@ egroups.com*

WriteBusiness *http://www.writebusiness.com*

Writers & Publishers Online Send a short summary to *submit@list-content.com*

Glossary

A full glossary is available at *http://www.e-business-essentials.com/essentials/glossary/htm*